THE

Cal-Der-Went

Walk

by

Geoffrey Carr

Maps by Geoffrey Carr.

TRAIL CREST PUBLICATIONS Ltd.,
- "from footprint to finished book."

1994

Sandia Mountains
New Mexico. USA

**TRAIL CREST
PUBLICATIONS
Ltd.,**
Milne House,
Speedwell Mill,
Miller's Green,
Wirksworth,
Derbyshire
DE4 4BL
☎
(0629) 826354
(0629) 826354

Edited, typeset, designed, paged, printed, marketed and distributed by John N. Merrill.

© Text, walks, Maps, & photographs
Geoffrey Carr 1994.

First Published   - July 1994.

ISBN 1 874754 26 8

*U.S.A.
office -
P.O. Box 124,
Santa Rosa,
New Mexico
88435
U.S.A.*

Please note - The maps in this guide are purely illustrative. You are encouraged to use the appropriate 1:25,000 O.S. map.

Meticulous research has been undertaken to ensure that this publication is highly accurate at the time of going to press. The publishers, however, cannot be held responsible for alterations, errors or omissions, but they would welcome notification of such for future editions.

Typeset in - Times - bold, italic and plain 9pt and 18pt.

Printed by - Footprint Press Ltd./John N. Merrill at
Milne House, Speedwell Mill, Miller's Green, Wirksworth,

Cover photogragh - Crossing Bull Clough by Geoffrey Carr.
© Geoffrey Carr. 1994.

An all British
product.

CONTENTS

Ladybower Reservoir at the southern end of the walk.

INTRODUCTION

The idea of a long distance walk connecting the valleys of the Calder and the Derwent came mainly from a basic need of such a walk in the West and South Yorkshire areas which was close enough to areas of population yet could still be classed as a country walk. Some of the inspiration came from the late A. Wainwright's 'Coast to Coast' walk, the guide book to which refers to the opportunity for other people to develop their own long distance routes. The 'Cal-Der-Went Walk' uses and connects existing footpaths and is now a recognised long distance route. It is now marked on the O.S. 1:50,000 Sheet 110 map

The walk was first completed in its entirety by members of the Ossett St. John's Methodist Church Walking Club in May 1978, after the route was surveyed by the author, Malcolm Blythe and the late Norman Jackson, who also took the photographs for the original edition of the book.

As can be seen from the map of the whole route, on page 6, the walk can be conveniently divided into four sections. The first section is through a wooded valley, three Nature Reserves and a country park. The second section explores the rolling farmland and hidden farmsteads of South Yorkshire and from Langsett there is a short moorland section, followed by a lake-side walk to the Snake Road in North Derbyshire.

The walk crosses the watersheds and the valleys of the Calder, Dearne, Don and Porter before arriving at the Derwent. In addition to the main watersheds, other minor ones are crossed to streams and tributaries of the Dearne.

Most of the way is on footpaths, with as little road walking as possible and with one short town section through Penistone. The roads not only give access for support teams but also allow the walk to be joined at various places en route.

There is much to see along the way and time can be spent looking at the birds in Bretton, where a large heronry has built up over the last few years and where in the spring and summer months migrant warblers stay to nest. Cannon Hall has a museum in which among other exhibits, there is the museum of the

13th./18th. Hussars. These and other places may induce some to linger but strong walkers will be able to complete the walk in one day. There is no intention of imposing a time limit and the walk may be done in either direction, bits of it being completed as time and inclination allow.

Those who complete the walk may apply for a completion card and rucksack badge but as prices change yearly, it is recommended the interested parties write to the Recorder for the latest circular before doing the walk. Please enclose a stamped addressed envelope.

The Recorder's address is -
The 'Cal-Der-Went Walk' Recorder
Fern Cottage,
Cardigan Lane,
Manor Road,
Ossett,
West Yorkshire
WF5 OLT

The walk may be done in either direction but the north to south route is described here. Anyone doing the walk in the opposite direction should have no difficulty in finding the way using the sketch maps provided. Also, the entire route may be followed on the O.S. 1:50000 Sheet No. 110 and a more detailed picture is obtained using the 1:25000 series sheets SE21/31 Horbury, SE20/30 Barnsley, SK18 Castleton and SK19 Derwent Dale.

Early starters at Horbury Bridge are asked to maintain a reasonable silence during the first half-mile of the walk, until all the houses have been passed. The community at Coxley should be treated in a similar manner.

Geoffrey Carr.
Ossett 1994.

The Cal-Der-Went Walk

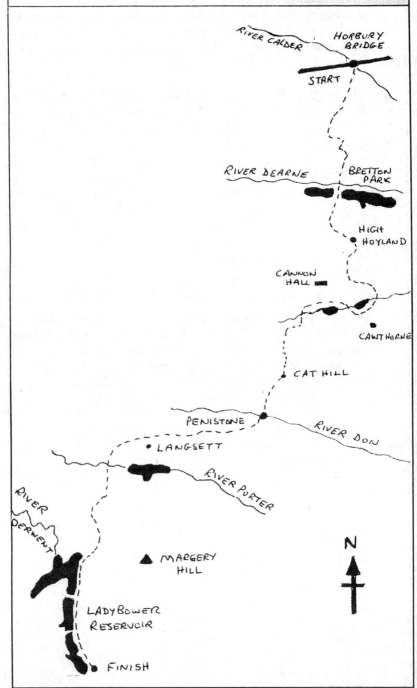

....

Congratulations on
completing

THE

CAL-DER-WENT

WALK

Date .... Time ....

This Completion card is available to all finishing the walk.

The rucksack badge illustrates the five rivers which are crossed during the traverse.

THE PIONEERS

The first Cal-Der-Went walkers at Horbury Bridge at the Start of the walk on May 20th.1978.

The Cal-Der-Went Walk was first completed in its entirety by fifteen walkers from the St.John's Methodist Church walking club,Ossett,West Yorkshire on May 20th.1978. The Club was formed in 1970 and took its full title from the Lyke Wake Walk which its members used to complete every year,usually sponsored for some charity or other. The author and originator of the Cal-Der-Went Walk is its Secretary.

On the inaugural crossing,the walkers were supported by a team of nine cooks and drivers led by the late Jim Smales.Jim was support team leader of the walking club and looked after the transport and feeding arrangements on the Club's long walks. He died suddenly on September 8th. 1979, a sad loss to his wife and family,the Church and the walking club. At the start of the walk,we had our photographs taken on the bridge over the River Calder at Horbury by Norman Jackson,who had recently done a solo unsupported crossing of the Lyke Wake Walk when he was well in his 60's. We left the Calder at 6.25 am and walked the well known footpaths through Coxley and alongside Stonycliff Wood, which is now a Nature Reserve administered by the Yorkshire Wildlife Trust.The footpaths through the woods are not rights of way and a permit is required from the Trust if one wishes to study birds in the area.

Stocks Moor,also a Nature Reserve,but with a public footpath across it was, as usual, quite muddy but good time was made to the road where the support team had prepared hot soup and tea.

We continued down the track towards Bretton Park where, after a short rest by the cascade bridge between the lakes,we trudged the uphill section to the lodge at the top.Walkers on this section may see the early morning training sessions for a string of race horses who use the gallops on most days.

Cawthorne Park provided us with the welcome sight of our supporters who had bacon,eggs and sausages sizzling on portable gas stoves. Suitably refreshed we tackled the agricultural country to the south west of Cawthorne, finding isolated farms in quiet valleys. One Mill Farm,still had the old water mill reasonably intact.The steep climb up Cat Hill to Netherlea farm and the flagged footpath soon brought us to Penistone.

One is soon through the town and out into the country again where an old, smelly refuse tip next to the footpath has now been landscaped.On across the fields and past Hartcliff Hill towards Langsett,where in the lay-by the support team had again worked wonders in providing a cooked dinner.We had done eighteen miles and had another twelve to go. After lunch,we crossed the River Little Don ,or Porter by the Brookhouse Bridge,following Cut Gate over the Moors.This was once called the Cart Gate,as merchants from the Woodlands Valley in Derbyshire used the route to transport their goods to the markets in Sheffield.

We dropped down towards Slippery Stones in the Derwent Valley and where the footpath sign pointed to Bamford,we started the last six miles along the east side of the three reservoirs now occupying the valley. The supporters had arrived at the end of the walk before we did, having enjoyed the drive on the ups and downs of the Strines road. We finished in 11 hour 20 minutes and the weather had been kind to us with sunshine most of the day.

The Club has repeated the walk on five more occasions. In May 1979, we used the South to North route,taking 12 hours,again in good weather. In 1982 the Club was heavily sponsored to do the Lyke Wake Walk,but owing to torrential rain the attempt was abandoned and we did the Cal-Der-Went Walk instead in October so that the members could earn some sponsor money.

The Club did the walk again in the years 1984,85 and in 1988,all of them being in aid of a charity. In the later years some of the 'old guard' were joined by new and younger members.

Members of St.John's Walking Club who have done The Cal-Der-Went Walk.
Roll of Honour.
Walkers.

Geoffrey Carr.	Anne Butcher.	Darren Darker.
Malcolm Blythe.	Wendy Mitchell	Jenny Murdoch.
Christopher Bowering.	Glenice Burrill.	Joanne Murdoch.
Peter Ward.	Ralph Round.	Leslie Jones.
Pat Ward.	Melvyn Bowering	Paul Blackburn.
Glyn Taylor.	Brian Noton.	Wayne Briggs.
Ken Butcher.	John Hallam.	Martin Sinar.
Barbara Butcher.	David Hendra.	Elsie Walton.
Maurice Simpson.	Gary Luck.	Christopher Quinn.
Keith Bradley.	Graeme Kent.	Frank Mitchell.
Janet Harrison	Norman Jackson.	Eddie Kent.
	Julie Pollard.	

Support Team Members

Jim Smales.	Norman Jackson.	Pat Round.
Joss Bowering.	Marian Carr.	Anne Blackburn.
Andrew Battye.	Ron Smith.	Mandy Marshall.
Molly Simpson.	Barbara Smith.	Ray England.
Joyce Battye.	Gill Hughes.	Rev.Derek Lund.
		Alan Smart

A Portrait Gallery of the St. John's Cal-Der-Went Walkers 1979

Malcolm Blythe.

The late Norman Jackson.

The author, Geoff Carr.

Marian Carr.

Maurice Simpson.

Molly Simpson.

A Portrait Gallery of the St. John's Cal-Der-Went Walkers 1979

Melvyn Bowering.

The late Chris. Bowering.

Joss Bowering.

Rev. Derek Lund.

Ron Smith.

Barbara Smith.

A Portrait Gallery of the St. John's Cal-Der-Went Walkers 1979

Ken Butcher.

The late Barbara Butcher.

Anne Butcher.

Janet Harrison.

Peter Ward.

Julie Pollard.

A Portrait Gallery of the St. John's Cal-Der-Went Walkers 1979

Wendy Mitchell.

Alan Smart.

Brian Noton.

Eddie Kent.

Ralph Round.

Pat Round.

A Portrait Gallery of the St. John's Cal-Der-Went Walkers 1979

John Hallam.

David Hendra.

Gill Hughes.

The people who followed.

1978 - Following the inaugural walk in 1978,two other groups completed the route in the same year. Mal Evans, Ralph Waude and four other teachers from the then Whitwood Mining and Technical College,Castleford finished in 10 hours 30 minutes and three staff from the New Hall Detention Centre at Flockton took just 10 hours,both groups walking north to south.

Many other groups and individuals have completed the walk in one or other direction,in the space of a day or in one or more sections over a period of time.The following compilation has been made from the comments received from those who have written to the Recorder for badges and certificates.

1979 - Messers Haigh,Taylor and Machin of the Wakefield C.H.A.,on a south to north route in April 1979, had drizzle and cross winds to contend with and were confused after the cricket field at Cawthorne, but otherwise concluded that the walk was good.

D.Allsop and a friend,from Hull,got lost on Stocks Moor in poor weather in May but also reckoned that they had a good day.

A month later,I.D.Intract and six friends from Sheffield crossed in 11 hours in a north to south direction,the writer of the report going to a chiropodist for blister treatment following their success. An unusual crossing was made by O.Dyson and company from British Steel,Stocksbridge,who walked from Penistone to the finish at Ladybower reservoir,caught trains and 'buses to Horbury and walked from there to Penistone.Reportedly having had a *"good day"*.

N.Huntley and eight friends from Keyingham,camped at Penistone and did the walk in two days in July.

Later in 1979,an avalanche of crossings took place with mass walks from the 12th Scouts,Wakefield, Waterton Rangers and Peglars Rambling Club, Doncaster.

G.Yates, I.Cooke and G.M.Garroch took 12 hours 30 minutes in October of that year,starting and finishing in darkness.

1980 - January 1980 saw the first winter crossing,with fifteen inches of snow over Cut Gate but the party led by Norman Haigh from Longwood Huddersfield still managed to finish in 11 hours 30 minutes. John Merrill,the long,long distance walker,came in March of that year with a party from Dronfield Rotary Club and turned in a time of 10 hour 15 minutes.

Ben Gunn of Rumbles Ramblers from Rotherham, did his second crossing of 1980 with their founder Frank Rumbles. Also, in that year, Stocksbridge High

School crossed and South Yorkshire Police made it one of their regular walks. Slazengers hockey team from Horbury crossed en-masse in July and twenty three pupils and teachers from Lepton Middle School took three days over the route.

Don Beeston and the N.C.B.'s Allerton Bywater Walking Club from Castleford walked across in 11 hours and enjoyed the experience. They were followed by Doncaster Hobblers, led by Alan Smith in 11 hours 20 mins. Other groups who completed the walk in 1980 were Batley Sports Centre, Huddersfield Rucksack Club, Yorkshire Purchasing Organisation, Leeds Skill Centre and many individuals like Ben Gunn who did a solo unsupported crossing.

Although it was never the intention that the walk would become a race for the fastest time, it was almost inevitable that speed merchants would enter the lists. Harry Machin was the first on September 7th. with a time of 5 hours 57 minutes.

1981 - started with a flourish with B.Hynes, John Needham, Paul Clegg and a friend from Sowerby Bridge. They walked from Dewsbury to the start, stayed overnight at Langsett and then from the end of the walk, walked to Hayfield to catch a train back to Sowerby Bridge.

Dewsbury Scouts crossed in just over 11 hours in March and Dewsbury C.H.A. Rambling Club took two days over the route, with Sheila Tolson looking in vain for a shed at the watershedding!

In April, Dr.G.Hulley from Sheffield lowered the fastest time to 4 hours 55 minutes, while J.R.Wadilove and M.Thompson of Harrogate walked both ways in four days.

Richard Pinkney and Hilary Sive came from Manchester and walked the north to south route while Wakefield Footpaths Group crossed in times between 10 and 12 hours.

Ken and Shirley Brown thought that the walk was more difficult than the Howarth Hobble and took two days to complete it, as did the York Hoboes. B.N.Brown came from Otley, walked to Ladybower and then hitched lifts back to Horbury.

Sharon Cox and Margo Crawford in a group from Hemsworth, slept in the taxi to the start and cried in Coxley.

Ben Gunn did his fourth crossing and a big party from Doncaster Wayfarers also completed the walk in the October of that year. Other groups doing the walk in 1981 were Waterton First School, a party from Lincoln, Carringtons of Dewsbury led by Bob White, Derby Rambling Association, a big party from Barnsley led by M.Reavill and individuals from Nottingham, Rothwell, Sheffield, Newcastle-on-Tyne and another group from Hemsworth.

1982 - G.and D.Hopkin were the first to do the walk in 1982 and later, South Yorkshire Police crossed again .

Selby Fell Walking Club did a north to south crossing in June led by R.Hudson and thought that the walk was a refreshing change from the Lyke Wake Walk and the White Rose Walk.

9th.Wakefield Scouts had a big party over in July and Eddie Noon and Graham Hodgson from Ben Shaws Walking and Stumbling Society crossed in 11 hours.

Cambridge University took up the challenge when, led by Colin Farrel,he and eleven others completed the walk in 8 hours 50 minutes.

Staff and pupils from the Rodillians School,Rothwell enjoyed their walk in October while D.Middlemass and G.Morl did the walk after completing the Calderdale Way and took 9 hours 40 minutes.

Other groups that year were from Kettering Hospital,Stocksbridge School, Pontefract Hospital and Rothwell Training Centre.

1983 - A group from Hull started 1983 off with a January crossing and found Langsett Moors under snow.They were followed by parties from Halifax, Wakefield and Dewsbury,all in the early months.

M.Peat led two others from Keighley on his second crossing and Rotherham Police and Scouts also did the walk in May.

Thornhill Scouts led by Tony and Allison Boothroyd raised £1,000 in sponsor money.

Waterton School from Wakefield took three outings to complete the crossing in June and D. and L. Sidwell used the route as a preparatory walk before doing the Lyke Wyke Walk later in the year.

Finally for 1983,Brean Robinson from Barton - on - Humber walked both ways in sections at the end of the year.

1984 - saw parties from the 54th.Sheffield Company of Boys Brigade, Skelmanthorpe,the Blisters Club from Barnsley Hospital,Stocksbridge School again,and the 9th.Wakefield Scouts. Bridget Mellor-Firth did a double crossing in August.

1985 - Ben Gunn did his sixth crossing in May 1985 and R.Skinner and B.Whiting of the Normanton Boot and Crutch Club took 10 hours 35 minute in August.

West Yorkshire Police,led by Ann Richardson,entered the lists in September and Anthony Fox, with the Wakefield Prison Striders, walked south to north in November.

The record for the fastest time was lowered again on December 12th. when Anthony Fox and P. Fenton clocked a time of 4 hours 46 minutes 52 seconds.Like Bill Cowley and the Lyke Wake Walk record,we refuse to accept seconds, so the record to date stands at 4 hours 47 minutes.

18

1986 - In March 1986,Terry Griffiths and the White Cross Walkers from Bolton On- Dearne found deep snow over Cut Gate and R.F.Robson with the Cockburn Ramblers and Pedestrians had snow all the way in the same month. Queen Street Social Club,Wakefield raised £500 for the Wakefield Disabled Sports Association in April,crossing north to south in 12 hours 30 minutes. Ewen F.N.Rennie,from Combs Hill School,crossed quickly in August and brought the record down to 4 hours 36 minutes on a north to south route. Steve Ashurst led a large group from the White Horse Inn,Sharlston,on July 27th.,everyone crossing in 10 to 12 hours.Rosehill Ramblers, Riccal Mine Walking Club and Thornhill Scouts were other groups crossing during the year.

1987 - The record was smashed again in 1987,when Stephen Robinson and Andrew Blanshard crossed in May in a time of 3 hours 58 minutes, stopping occasionally to look at the views,they said! This time still stands as the all-time record for a reported crossing in a north to south direction. Stocksbridge School came again to do the walk and Janet Underwood came from Danbury in Essex and did a solo unsupported crossing,south to north in 10 hours 50 minutes. Mark Elam and five others from Went Vale School ,Pontefract,camped out on Margery Hill in September and completed the walk the next day.

1988 - In 1988,Bolton Ramblers Association brought a large party in January and February when they re-named the second section,the Cal-Der WET Walk,because it rained the whole day.Peter Sleightholm and Margaret Griffiths did their second crossing with this group. Richard Collier's 3rd.crossing was done on April 1st. with a party from Rothwell and Joyce and John Tagg headed a large group from Barnsley on May 1st.,with a time of 9 hours 59 minutes. West Yorkshire Police made another crossing as did Rodillians School, while other parties included Burton Wood First School,South Kirkby; Yorkshire Tykes Walking Club, Batley,led by Paul Eyles;Yorkshire Bank Walking Club and Went Vale School again,this time camping at Langsett.

1989 - Frank Mitchell did a solo unsupported crossing in May 1989 in 14 hours 20 minutes,using the experience gained on an earlier Lyke Wake Walk. Other groups in 1989 were The Edward Sheerian School Barnsley; Dewsbury Scouts;Wilkinson Home and Garden Stores, Worksop and West Yorkshire Police again,led by PC.Graham Leighton . Martin Wilcox from Sheffield was the youngest to do the walk in one go.He was eight years old.

1990 - In 1990,the 17th.Outwood Church Scouts had a big party over the walk in April,walking North to South, as did the Pegasus Youth Club Horbury but they walked south to north.

Sheila Tolson was over again in July, reputedly to be still looking for that shed!

R.W.Ramsey and five Scouts from the Atlantis V.S.U.,South Wirral,took 13 hours 45 minutes on a north to south traverse.

1991 - R.and J.Turner.M.and S. Briggs, C. and G.Jones from Upper Cumberworth started the 1991 season by walking north to south in January, while the next party was Dave Gill and the Mitchell Laithes Sewage Treatment Works Ramblers, who completed the walk in April,walking south to north in just over 14 hours.

G.M.Pye came from Essex (staying at his parents house in Ossett) and did the route solo and unsupported in 10 hours 45 minutes.

Nottingham Police led by David Shardlow turned in a time of 10 hours in July.

1992 - The first group to report in 1992 were West Yorkshire Police,who crossed again in May,with Paul McMahon crossing in 8 hours 3 minutes. Other parties from Huddersfield,Rotherham,Wombwell Town Link,led by Andrew Kelly,and Warlocks Venture Scouts also did the walk.The last group came from Wellington,Somerset and slept overnight in the Scout hut in Ossett.

1993 - This year started with a party from Wakefield in March followed by S.Baldwin who headed a group from Huddersfield in April. Wakefield Footpaths Group crossed in May,turning in some good times and a party led by K.Isaac from Wakefield Grammar School crossed in June over a period of two days.

One of the last to do the walk was Douglas Haigh, who led David Baker and Wendy Mulheir from Wakefield on a north to south route, unsupported, on November 28th. in 9 hrs. 15 mins.

Walkers crossing Brookhouse Bridge over the River Porter on the first "Cal-Der-Went Walk."

Calder Valley to Cawthorne Park
- 9 miles.

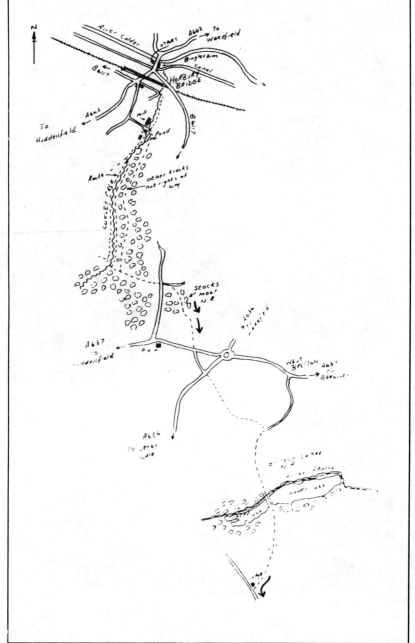

Stage 1.
Calder Valley to
Cawthorne Park
- 9 miles

Map -1:25,000 Pathfinder Series Sheet No. SE21/31 Horbury.

The start of the walk is on the bridge over the river Calder by the Bingley Arms Hotel, in the village of Horbury Bridge near Wakefield, on the A642 Wakefield - Huddersfield Road. Walk towards Huddersfield, under the railway arches, and turn left on Water Lane by the off-licence shop. Follow Water Lane until it bends round to the right, then continue down the narrow footpath with the stream at the right hand side. Follow the stream up the valley for about half a mile to arrive at the small community of Coxley.

Turn right by the mill and then turn left after passing a row of houses. Turn left again, behind the row of houses and go down to the small lake. Now turn right along the valley bottom, with a high wall on the right and a wire mesh fence on the left. Continue southwards, following the stream with the wood on the left and fields on the right. Cross several stiles until, at the end of the last field, the path meets a broad track running left to right. Turn left here, go over a foot bridge and climb uphill until the main road is reached - this is the B6117. (There are other footpaths through the woods which are used more than the route described, but these are not rights-of-way).

Cross the road and continue down the road opposite, then turn right on the first obvious footpath and cross Stocksmoor Common on the public footpath. Ignore the stiles and keep outside the fences until the southern edge of the reserve is reached. Go over the stile here, or through the gate alongside it, and up the track to the A637. Cross this road and continue along the road opposite. Cross the next main road, the A636, and go along the broad track opposite until a big iron gate is reached. Go through the gate and along the track towards Bretton Park. Turn right after going through the wooden gate and on through the next gate, also a wooden one. The track now continues downhill passing through another iron gate to Cascade Bridge between the two lakes.

Now go forward, without changing direction, through the big iron gate, and, after a long pull uphill to the lodge, yet another iron gate is met. Do not go through this one but use the style at the left-hand side.

Calder Valley to Cawthorne Park - 9 miles.

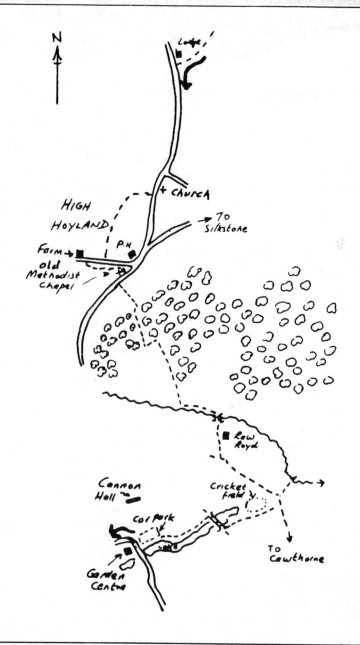

N

Lodge

+ CHURCH

HIGH HOYLAND

To Silkstone

P.H

Farm →

Old Methodist Chapel

Low Royd

Cannon Hall

Cricket field

Car Park

To Cawthorne

Garden Centre

Turn left up the road and after another long uphill trudge, go past High Hoyland church, which is now an activity centre and turn right on a footpath at the beginning of a line of yew trees, marked as a "Public Bridleway." Follow the footpath as it swings to the left and with a low stone wall and a steeply banked wood on the right, continue to a road. Turn right and walk on the road towards Winter Hill Farm, about 200 yards ahead. A footpath immediately opposite the farm slants down to the left and through a wooded area.

Go through the five-barred gate, or use the stile at the side, and pass in front of two houses. Walk to the right, down the broad tarmaced drive and turn left at the public footpath sign, through another wood. The path leads downhill to a wooden gate. Go through this and out on to the road.

Turn right and after passing, on the right, what was High Hoyland Methodist Chapel, still recognisable from its architecture, turn left over a stile and take the footpath across a field and into a wood. Follow the track southwards through the wood and go over a stile into a field. Once over the stile, it is better to turn left and walk round the edge of the field to join a broad farm track heading south towards Cawthorne. Turn left by a stream and then take the second gate on the right passing 'Raw Royd'. This was a ruin and is marked on the O.S. maps but is now demolished. When another track is reached running left to right, turn left over a stile, cross another stream by a bridge and follow the track that leads up to Cawthorne village. 'Cal-Der-Went' walkers, however, must soon turn right over another bridge and go through a swing gate and past a cricket field. Make for the bridge over the park lake. Once over the bridge turn left and walk along the lake side, making for the car park which can be seen ahead through the trees.

The route through the park is not a right-of-way but is well used by visitors to Cannon Hall and the lakes. The car park here, alongside the lake, makes a good place for a support team to meet the walkers. It is, at the time of going to press, a pay and display car-park, but toilet facilities are available here and sometimes a refreshment van operates, a useful aid to non-supported walkers.

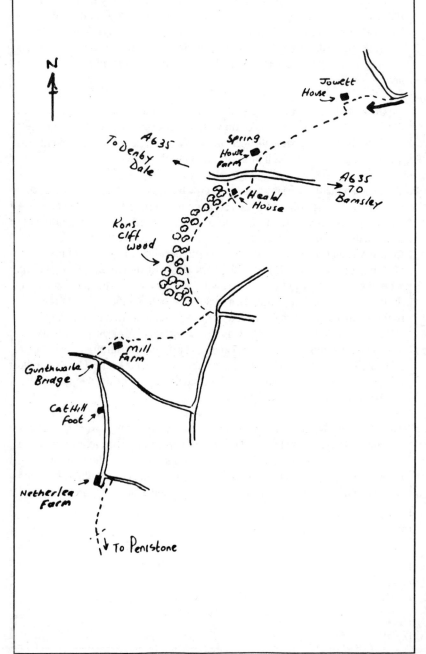

Stage 2.
Cawthorne
to Langsett
- 9 miles

Map - 1:25,000 Pathfinder Series Sheet No. SE20/30 - Barnsley.

From the car park, the walk continues westward along the road with the garden centre on the left. Leave the road at a public footpath sign to Jowett House Farm. A circular construction on the right by a tree is Jowett House Spa, the water from which, the locals believe, has medicinal properties. The path goes between the farm buildings and then left along a walled lane. When the lane enters a field, turn right with the hedge on the right hand side. Go over four stiles and across a field to Spring House Farm. When the initial exploration for the walk was carried out in August 1977, there was a cereal crop in the field but the path had been well trodden. In any case, keep in a single file when crossing this and other fields. The farm road leads to a main road, the A635. Cross this turn right for a few yards and follow the public footpath sign on the left. The path bends left and then right between farm buildings to a stream.

Go over a wooden bridge, up the steep bank opposite and turn right at the top. Amongst the brambles is a stone stile and beyond it a wooden stile. Cross both these and head for Heald House seen in the immediate distance. Go past the house and into the lane, turn left but almost at once slant down to the right and follow the path along the steeply wooded Rons Cliff. Keep to the edge of the wood with a wall on the left. At the end of the wood the track swings left but the walk goes through a gate on the right and across the field on a bearing of 240° until a wall is reached.

Follow the wall round to the left until a stile is reached at the wall corner. Go over this, turn right and follow the field edge, which has an area of scrub and low bushes on the right, until a second stile is found in the wall. Go over this stile and follow a track down to Mill Farm. Go around the farm on a signposted route and out on the farm road beyond. This road leads to Gunthwaite Bridge which can be seen from it and which may be reached by an obvious stile. Go over the bridge and take the road to the right up to Cat Hill and Netherlea Farm.

Climb to the top of the road and then turn left on Firs Lane. Turn right on the first footpath after passing the farm buildings and head for a stile in the wall

Cawthorne to Langsett - 9 miles.

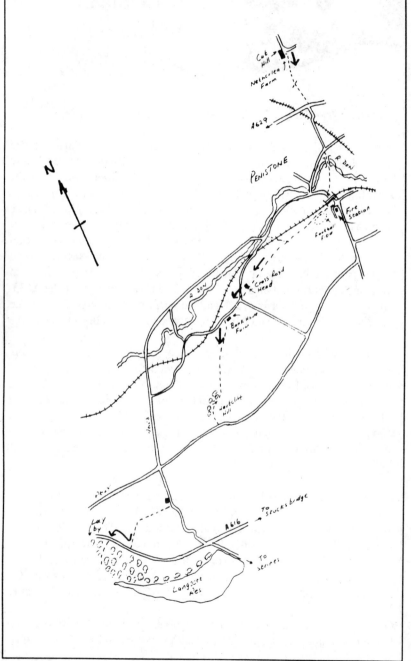

opposite and then on a 210° bearing to another stile in the next wall. A due south bearing from here will lead to a small swing gate, beyond which is a flagged path leading to the main Barnsley road, the A629. Cross the road and go down Wellhouse Lane towards Penistone. At the bottom of Wellhouse Lane take the lane opposite and cross the Don river (here unpolluted) and continue straight forward, eventually going between houses and on to a main road in Penistone. Turn left, go under the railway bridge and take the next road on the right. This road eventually passes the fire station but the walkers must turn right on Stottercliffe Road, passing a football field on the left and with the electrified railway on the right.

The main footpath carries straight on towards the railway but Cal-Der-Went walkers should turn left and head for the stile opposite. On an almost due west bearing, the track crosses several fields and stiles to Cross Royd Head Farm. Go over the stile and down the farm road, turning left at the end. Take the next road to the right as far as Bank House Farm, when the next footpath on the left must be followed. This is a broad track narrowing after passing over a stile by a gate. Follow the wall side to a wooded bank and continue on a path by the wood edge with Hartcliffe Hill on the left.

Turn right at the road and left at the cross roads towards Langsett. After passing the last house on the right, turn right along a broad track. This eventually leads to the A616 Sheffield - Manchester road where soon after turning right a lay by is reached. This makes a good support point and a starting point for the next section, even more so now as there is a large car-parking area just behind it.

Mill Farm from second stile.

Langsett to the Derwent - 12 miles

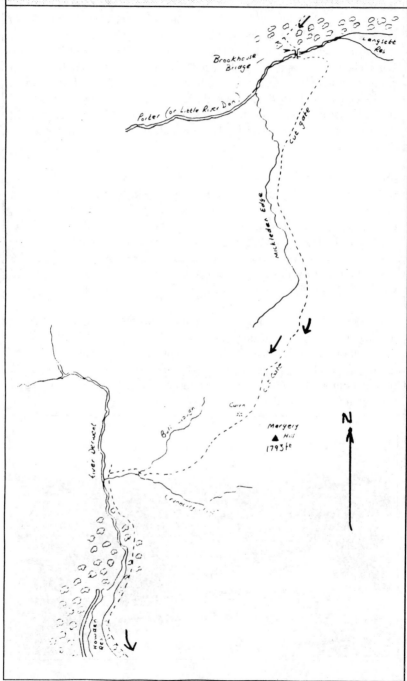

Stage 3.
Langsett to
the Derwent
- 12 miles

Map - 1:25,000 Pathfinder Series Sheet No. SK18 - Castleton and SK19 Derwent Dale.

This is the longest section of the walk and is by far the wildest, reaching 1,700 ft. above sea level at the highest point with no point of access between the Sheffield - Manchester road and the head of Howden Reservoir in the Derwent Valley.

From the lay-by on the A616, cross the road and walk back a few yards to a gate, go through the gate and follow the track until it divides. Take the left hand track, sign-posted 'Derwent', which soon leads to the Porter or Little Don river, spanned by Brookhouse bridge. Over the bridge the track now goes left but soon swings round right to reach a point high above the bridge. The footpath has been diverted here to prevent further erosion taking place.

The footpath continues southwards, with Mickleden Beck down to the right. Mickleden Edge became famous for a while in May 1982, Britain's first Marmora's Warbler took up temporary residence in the heather, and was "twitched" by bird watchers from all over Britain. The author came to see it and made a television debut when interviewed by the B.B.C.'s *"Look North"* team.

The path, marked Cut Gate on the maps, heads in a southerly direction, is easy to find and is well used by walkers. After about three miles, the watershed is reached and at the summit one is rewarded with fine views down into the Derwent Valley. The descent is steeper down a cairned track to the steep side of Bull Clough. The path then swings to the side of Cranberry Clough down to the confluence of the two streams. Cross Bull Clough here and continue down the right hand side of the stream. Sign-posts are plentiful so follow the one marked 'Derwent and Bamford', going over the foot bridge and along the broad track at the east side of the three reservoirs.

The reservoirs in the Derwent Valley were also famous for a while. During the 1939-45 war, they were used by the R.A.F.'s *"Dam Buster"* squadron as training for the attack on the dams in Germany. Anniversary fly-pasts have

Langsett to the Derwent - 12 miles

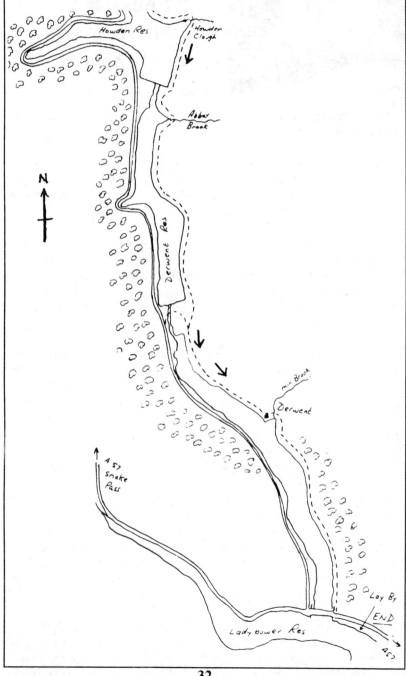

also been made in recent years and these usually attract large crowds of onlookers Also, during the flooding of this valley, Derwent village had to be abandoned and at times of drought, some of the ruins of the village can be seen in the shallow water. This event brings the crowds as well. Derwent bridge was removed from the old village before it disappeared under water and was re-built at the top end of the valley at Slippery Stones.

The track becomes a metalled road for a while but reverts to a track again beyond a car park. Go down to the bridge on the Snake Road and to the end of the 'Cal-Der-Went Walk'.

Derwent Bridge (Slippery Stones) in the upper Derwent valley.

View from Spring House Farm. The track passes between two farm buildings, up the bank and across to Heald House in the distance.

Support team and walkers at lay-by near Langsett.

The South to North Route

The obvious direction of the walk is north to south, Calder to the Derwent, but there are no objections to the walk being done in the opposite direction.

There are however one or two places where care is needed to avoid getting off course. The first of these is just beyond the top of Howden Reservoir where one takes the steep path out of the valley. Keep Bull Clough on the left and Cranberry Clough on the right and follow sign-post marked Flouch. The energetic might detour to take in Margery Hill, away to the east.

Secondly, in Penistone turn right between houses after passing under the railway bridge.

Thirdly, when approaching Netherlea Farm, turn left onto Firs Lane and then turn right down the road.

Fourthly, after crossing Stocks Moor, go down the old colliery road but fork right down a narrow metalled track. Continue downhill, over the foot-bridge and turn right by an obvious gate-post. The path follows the edge of the wood, with fields on the left. In places it follows the meanderings of the stream. Continue along the valley bottom, passing the small lake on the right and the wall on the left. At the end of the wall, turn left by the back of the cottages and then right out onto the metalled road. Turn right again and then left by the mill. A broad track leads on to Water Lane. Turn right on to the main road under the arches and onto the bridge over the River Calder and the end of the walk.

South to north walking may appeal to some as there is ample refreshment available nearby, as long as you choose the right time to finish the walk. Don't expect or ask for refreshment after normal closing time.

High Hoyland church.

Cannon Hall, Cawthorne.

Observe the Country Code -

1. Guard against fire risks.
2. Fasten all gates.
3. Keep dogs under proper control.
4. Keep to the paths across farm land.
5. Avoid damage to fences, hedges and walls.
6. Leave no litter.
7. Safeguard water supplies.
8. Protect wild life, wild plants and trees.
9. Go carefully on country roads.
10. Respect the life of the countryside.

If you wish to explore the Nature Reserves at Stocksmoor and Bretton Lakes, away from the public rights-of-way, please write for a permit to the Yorkshire Naturalist's Trust, 20 Castlegate, York YOI IRP.

Remember that the track over the moorland section reaches a height of 1,700 ft. above sea level and that a drizzle in the valley can be a blizzard on Margery Hill. If you walk in winter, go prepared.

Overnight accommodation is available at 'The Crown' in Penistone; Bank view Cafe at Langsett provides meals and has camping facilities. Mitchell's Camp site at Middlestown near the northern end of the walk also has camping and Millhouse Camping Barn ,near Penistone, also provides beds and meals. Telephone Ken or Pat on 0226 762917 for details.

Walkers should note that part of the moorland section may be closed during the grouse shooting season and all restrictions should be observed.Footpaths will always be open but access to the moors may be stopped. Also in very dry summers,even the rights of way may be suspended in order to reduce the risk of fire. Certificates and badges will not be supplied to walkers crossing the moorland section when closure restrictions are in force.

Limited parking is available in the lay-by at the end of the walk on the A57. Anyone wishing to park on the road leading to the Derwent valley,should first obtain permission from the Severn Trent Water.

Acknowledgements

Many people have contributed to the success of the walk and my thanks are due to the following:

To the late Norman Jackson, some of whose photographs are used in this book.

To Malcolm Blythe, who walked the whole route with me during the planning stages and who read the proofs.

To the late Jim Smales, who led the support team until his untimely death and was a tower of strength on all the Club's ventures.

To Bill Morris, who helped to sort out footpath problems in the South Yorkshire area.

And finally to all the members of the St.John's Methodist Church walking club, who did the inaugural walk and have helped in many ways with their enthusiasm and encouragement.

Crossing Bull Clough at its junction with Cranberry Clough.

"from footprint to finished book"

OTHER BOOKS by John N. Merrill Published by TRAIL CREST PUBLICATIONS Ltd.

CIRCULAR WALK GUIDES -

SHORT CIRCULAR WALKS IN THE PEAK DISTRICT - Vol. 1 and 2
CIRCULAR WALKS IN WESTERN PEAKLAND
SHORT CIRCULAR WALKS IN THE STAFFORDSHIRE MOORLANDS
SHORT CIRCULAR WALKS - TOWNS & VILLAGES OF THE PEAK DISTRICT
SHORT CIRCULAR WALKS AROUND MATLOCK
SHORT CIRCULAR WALKS IN THE DUKERIES
SHORT CIRCULAR WALKS IN SOUTH YORKSHIRE
SHORT CIRCULAR WALKS IN SOUTH DERBYSHIRE
SHORT CIRCULAR WALKS AROUND BUXTON
SHORT CIRCULAR WALKS AROUND WIRKSWORTH
SHORT CIRCULAR WALKS IN THE HOPE VALLEY
40 SHORT CIRCULAR WALKS IN THE PEAK DISTRICT
CIRCULAR WALKS ON KINDER & BLEAKLOW
SHORT CIRCULAR WALKS IN SOUTH NOTTINGHAMSHIRE
SHIRT CIRCULAR WALKS IN CHESHIRE
SHORT CIRCULAR WALKS IN WEST YORKSHIRE
CIRCULAR WALKS TO PEAK DISTRICT AIRCRAFT WRECKS by John Mason
CIRCULAR WALKS IN THE DERBYSHIRE DALES
SHORT CIRCULAR WALKS IN EAST DEVON
SHORT CIRCULAR WALKS AROUND HARROGATE
SHORT CIRCULAR WALKS IN CHARNWOOD FOREST
SHORT CIRCULAR WALKS AROUND CHESTERFIELD
SHORT CIRCULAR WALKS IN THE YORKS DALES - Vol 1 - Southern area.
SHORT CIRCULAR WALKS IN THE AMBER VALLEY (Derbyshire)
SHORT CIRCULAR WALKS IN THE LAKE DISTRICT
SHORT CIRCULAR WALKS IN THE NORTH YORKSHIRE MOORS
SHORT CIRCULAR WALKS IN EAST STAFFORDSHIRE
DRIVING TO WALK - 16 Short Circular walks south of London by Dr. Simon Archer
LONG CIRCULAR WALKS IN THE PEAK DISTRICT - Vol.1 and 2.
LONG CIRCULAR WALKS IN THE STAFFORDSHIRE MOORLANDS
LONG CIRCULAR WALKS IN CHESHIRE
WALKING THE TISSINGTON TRAIL
WALKING THE HIGH PEAK TRAIL
WALKING THE MONSAL TRAIL & OTHER DERBYSHIRE TRAILS

CANAL WALKS -

VOL 1 - DERBYSHIRE & NOTTINGHAMSHIRE
VOL 2 - CHESHIRE & STAFFORDSHIRE
VOL 3 - STAFFORDSHIRE
VOL 4 - THE CHESHIRE RING
VOL 5 - LINCOLNSHIRE & NOTTINGHAMSHIRE
VOL 6 - SOUTH YORKSHIRE
VOL 7 - THE TRENT & MERSEY CANAL

JOHN MERRILL DAY CHALLENGE WALKS -

WHITE PEAK CHALLENGE WALK
DARK PEAK CHALLENGE WALK
PEAK DISTRICT END TO END WALKS
STAFFORDSHIRE MOORLANDS CHALLENGE WALK
THE LITTLE JOHN CHALLENGE WALK

YORKSHIRE DALES CHALLENGE WALK
NORTH YORKSHIRE MOORS CHALLENGE WALK
LAKELAND CHALLENGE WALK
THE RUTLAND WATER CHALLENGE WALK
MALVERN HILLS CHALLENGE WALK
THE SALTER'S WAY
THE SNOWDON CHALLENGE
CHARNWOOD FOREST CHALLENGE WALK
THREE COUNTIES CHALLENGE WALK (Peak District).
CAL-DER-WENT WALK by Geoffrey Carr,
THE QUANTOCK WAY

INSTRUCTION & RECORD -
HIKE TO BE FIT.....STROLLING WITH JOHN
THE JOHN MERRILL WALK RECORD BOOK

MULTIPLE DAY WALKS -
THE RIVERS'S WAY
PEAK DISTRICT: HIGH LEVEL ROUTE
PEAK DISTRICT MARATHONS
THE LIMEY WAY
THE PEAKLAND WAY

COAST WALKS & NATIONAL TRAILS -
ISLE OF WIGHT COAST PATH
PEMBROKESHIRE COAST PATH
THE CLEVELAND WAY
WALKING ANGELSEY'S COASTLINE.

CYCLING Compiled by Arnold Robinson.
CYCLING AROUND THE NORTH YORK MOORS
CYCLING AROUND CASTLETON & the Hope Valley.

PEAK DISTRICT HISTORICAL GUIDES -
A to Z GUIDE OF THE PEAK DISTRICT
DERBYSHIRE INNS - an A to Z guide
HALLS AND CASTLES OF THE PEAK DISTRICT & DERBYSHIRE
TOURING THE PEAK DISTRICT & DERBYSHIRE BY CAR
DERBYSHIRE FOLKLORE
PUNISHMENT IN DERBYSHIRE
CUSTOMS OF THE PEAK DISTRICT & DERBYSHIRE
WINSTER - a souvenir guide
ARKWRIGHT OF CROMFORD
LEGENDS OF DERBYSHIRE
DERBYSHIRE FACTS & RECORDS
TALES FROM THE MINES by Geoffrey Carr
PEAK DISTRICT PLACE NAMES by Martin Spray

for a free copy
of the
**John Merrill
Walk Guide**
Catalogue
write to -
Trail Crest Publications Ltd.,

JOHN MERRILL'S MAJOR WALKS -
TURN RIGHT AT LAND'S END
WITH MUSTARD ON MY BACK
TURN RIGHT AT DEATH VALLEY
EMERALD COAST WALK

SKETCH BOOKS -
SKETCHES OF THE PEAK DISTRICT

COLOUR BOOK:-
THE PEAK DISTRICT.......something to remember her by.

OVERSEAS GUIDES -
HIKING IN NEW MEXICO - Vol 1 - The Sandia and Manzano Mountains.
Vol 2 - Hiking "Billy the Kid" Country. Vol 4 - N.W. area - " Hiking Indian Country."
"WALKING IN DRACULA COUNTRY" - Romania.

VISITOR'S GUIDES -
MATLOCK. BAKEWELL. ASHBOURNE.